Verses unveiled: A poetic collection

Dr Rajashree Pawar

BookLeaf
Publishing

India | USA | UK

Presentation by *BookLeaf Publishing*

Web: www.bookleafpub.com

E-mail: info@bookleafpub.com

ISBN:9789360948955

First edition 2024

DEDICATION

This collection,"Verses Unveiled: A poetic collection" is dedicated to my parents Mrs Bharati N. Akhargekar and Mr N G Akhargekar.

Your presence, resilience, and vibrant spirit have been the ink that colours these pages. May these verses be a reflection of the beauty you bring to the world.

With deepest admiration and gratitude,

Dr Rajashree Vivek Pawar

ACKNOWLEDGEMENT

In crafting "Verses Unveiled: A poetic collection" is dedicated to you.
I am indebted to the myriad influences that have shaped this collection. To the muses that stirred my creativity and the emotions that found their voice in verse, thank you for the inspiration.

I want to take this moment to thank everyone who supported and believed in this poetic endeavour. To my better half Dr. Vivek. S. Pawar, Mr and Mrs Rachita Rajendra Mirajkar, to my son Yash Pawar whose unwavering encouragement provided the foundation for these verses to blossom, I am truly thankful.

Special appreciation goes to the readers who embark on this poetic journey—may these words resonate with your hearts.

I want to thank the publisher who lent their expertise in enhancing the beauty of my book. Your contributions are invaluable.

Ultimately, this collection is a tapestry woven with threads of shared human experiences. To everyone who has played a role, big or small, in

bringing "Verses Unveiled: A poetic collection"
is dedicated to you.

To life, my deepest appreciation.

With gratitude,

Dr. Rajashree Vivek Pawar

PREFACE

In the delicate dance between words and emotions, "Verses Unveiled:A poetic collection" unfolds as a tapestry of the human experience. Through the rhythmic cadence of verses, we embark on a journey where sentiments find solace, and reflections paint vivid portraits of our shared existence.

These poems, like fragments of a soul laid bare, traverse the realms of love, loss, resilience, and the profound beauty inherent in our everyday moments. Within these pages, the language of the heart is translated into verses that resonate, inviting readers to explore the depths of their own emotions.

As the poet, my intention is not merely to convey thoughts but to create a sanctuary where words become vessels for the profound and the sublime. Each poem is a brushstroke, adding hues to the canvas of human connection, where readers may find echoes of their own stories.

May this collection serve as a companion, offering solace to those navigating the labyrinth of emotions and inspiring a celebration of the exquisite poetry embedded in the fabric of life.

Table of Content

RIVERSIDE SERENADE

Pedalling along the river, watching the water dance,
earth and water duet in rhythmic trance.
Rise and fall, serene ballet of the gasty wave,
where ships and boats dodge each other to save.

Sun peeping to kiss the golden water,
showering its love in ripples that shimmer and falter.
Water leaps on to the mossy stones releasing foam,
creatures enjoying bubbles in their comfort zone.

Sun splashes its golden glow on water's canvas,
painting natural masterpieces, flawless and
gorgeous.
Each wavelet weaves poem in the serenade of time,
singing and whispering with the stars in the celestial
rhyme.

Stingray and Catfish are guardians of the river,
whispering patrolling in the current together.
In soft moonlight glow many poetries weave,
of valour till night leaves.

Night falls the moonlight's shimmer reflecting
celestial dream,
casting an ethereal glow into a nocturnal scene.
Stars witness the river side serenade
whispering the natures story, as they parade.

Under the moon's soft glimmer, by the riverside,
a nocturnal whisper, where dreams ride.
Melodies of nature, in tranquil sprayed,
affection's rhythm, in a riverside serenade.

On sandy paths where dreams take flight,
awakening to the riverside's sheer delight.
Fulfilling dreams in nature's stride,
spirit soaring high with the riverside as guide.

In silent hush, stars guide the stream,
whispering tales, an ageless dream.
Moon in a dance of hide and seek,
a riverside serenade, enchantingly unique.

GIFT OF BLOOMING PERSONALITY

Life's garden adorned with diverse flowers,
each personality, a unique power.
Colours vibrant, each hue bespoke,
in brightness unique, a personality cloak.

With each bloom, a wonder unfurls,
enhancing the garden, stories whirl.
Every individual with personalities rare,
in knowing hearts, amazement flares.

In this wonderful world, a beautiful gift unfolds,
a blooming personality, a saga untold.
People of different mindset, in hues divine,
touching hearts rudely and softly, which cannot
decline.

Audacity blooms, facing gales in life.
resilient spirits, facing all surprise to dive.
Aroma of empathy whirl in the air,
dress of compassion and gratitude everyone wears.

Wisdom elevates, unfolding with age,
each experience engraves life's cherished page.
Colour of moral, virtues in the air,
master stroke of character in everyone's flare.

In life's poetry, vibrant hues spread,
personality blooms, a joyous path ahead.
Good personality a priceless gift,
everyone treasures with high spirit uplift.

Life's theatre, each soul plays their role,
with beautiful masquerade on the face.
Chasing their destiny, to achieve elusive goals
endless strides echo where ambition strolls.

Every individual unique and rare,
composition of character beyond compare.
On life's grand stage, each plays a part,
a masterpiece engraved on each heart.

BEAUTIFUL CREATION - WOMEN'S ELEGANCE

*In the kingdom of existence, a woman emerges,
elegant creation,
sculpture of wisdom, grace, resilience and
dedication.*

*Her vibrant smile, paints life with hues of joy,
creating a masterpiece that time can't destroy.*

*Her eyes filled with radiant dreams,
overcoming all hurdles like ice cream.*

*Strength and tolerance, a timeless creation,
her resilience through storm, a persistent foundation.*

*Mother, daughter, wife, sisters, radiant roles she
plays,
weaving success in every role that she sways.*

*Underestimated, yet blossoms, unwavering and tall,
knowing her potential to achieve everything, breaking
the wall.*

*She walks with grace, a portrait of fortitude,
where elegance never loses her gentle attitude.*

*Through trial and victory, her juggling so divine,
projecting perseverance in every line.*

*With every step, she paints her world with different
hues,
a portrait of confidence framed in self-assurance
never loses.*

*Her words, like pearls, looks serene, striving
excellence,
a magnificent creation—woman's elegance*

*In gentleness, a reservoir of might,
understanding hearts, a comforting light.*

*A resilient spirit, to be admired,
enduring strength, in challenges, inspired.*

*Elegance resides within laughter's embrace,
kindness flowing with a gentle trace.*

*Understanding all with a touch of grace,
in the dance of life, a charming pace.*

HER BEAUTY THROUGH MY EYES

On the canvas of perception, her beauty through my
eyes,
graceful movement, where admiration lies.

Her deep blue eyes, a tranquil ocean's reflection,
whispering waves, an ethereal connection.

Her smile, canvas of joys unfurled,
creating a rainbow that lights the world.

Beautiful rose in garden of eden, petals of grace,
In nature's cuddle, a delicate dance takes place.

She is beauty with brains, a harmonious blend,
crafted with elegance, and wisdom, a journey without
end.

Luminating dreams created, where dreams are born,
in the soft glow of hope, a radiant dawn is sworn.

Her presence makes time a fleeting rhyme,
memories dance with grace, a timeless chime.

With each heartbeat, a tale unfolds,
echoes of life a rhythmic journey moulds.

Her beauty through my eyes, an eternal saga,
on the stage of admiration, a perpetual drama.

PINNACLE PURSUITS: VERSES OF ATHLETIC VALOUR

Domain where valour meets the field,
Athletes sweat, the destiny revealed.
A symphony of noise, a dance of cheers,
where dreams of athletics take flight without fear.

In the pool's cradle, swimmers sail,
freestyle in the aquatic tale.
As they grow, achievements scale,
their skills they unveil.

Gravity fails when gymnasts perform their flips,
and appreciation lies on people's lips.
Acrobatic, cart wheel, artistic gymnastic trance,
in every move they shine in a rhythmic glance.

Battlefield of 64 white and black squares,
pawns march calculated everywhere.
Checkmate, slatemate the only hope,
victory on the chessboard cannot escape.

Kabaddi kabaddi on the field, warriors take flight,
the tale of defenders and raiders in the light. Ignite.
A combative sport, skills, speed and grace,
breathtaking expression on the face.

From dusty to verdent ground,
cricket symphony in every corner found.
The bowler's spin catches soar in flight
Nation's cheers echo pure sporting light.

Cycling, rhythmic journey through hills and valleys.
pedals and wheels spin in harmony at the finale.
Thrills glide, excitement takes its height,
nature whispers the adventures delight.

On the mat, wrestler symphony begins,
muscles against muscles exhibiting strength to win.
In the world of wrestling, determination strides,
overcoming every challenge, where true glory
resides.

Hockey stick in constant debate,
dribbling the ball on estatough as players strike with
fate.
When ball embraces the net cheers echo awesome,
in the fast paced game where passion blossoms.

In blades' ballet, a rhythmic art,
Gatka unfolds, a warrior's heart.
Swift and steady, the sticks command,
powerful skills across the land.

In the arena, where athlete's perform might,
their prowess unfolds to take flight.
On the pinnacle of pursuit, victory unfurl,
dreams ascend, in valour that swirls.

TREES : OUR BEST FRIENDS

In forest deep, nature's special gift, trees,
friendship among green trees whisper tales of bees.
Their branches reach, a leafy play,
sunlight's spotlight, a radiant display.

In the forest apothecary, trees whisper medicine,
in nature's book, a sacred place.
In joys and pain they stand tall guarding true,
protecting mother Earth, their steadyfast view.

Every season they stand, resilient and strong,
spreading their arms, a floral envelope.
Giving us life, a gift profound,
trees breathe life, hope is found.

In nature's anthem, a plea we send
Save trees, save forests, let their legacy trend.
Creating, canopy of care, where dreams are born,
in nature's embrace, hopes adorn.

Trees our friend in every guise, a bond so strong,
unspoken, enduring forever they belong.
Let us cherish, in every leaf's embrace,
the friendship of trees, a timeless grace.

ODE TO THE EARTH

Ode to the Earth, our splendid home,
green carpet beneath the vast blue dome.
Mountains soaring, our pride held high,
Oceans wide, nature's gift from the sky.

In this amazing realm, a divine creation,
nature's wonders, a breathtaking narration.
God's gift, a treasure of boundless worth,
Ode to the Earth, our beautiful birth.

A planet unique, beauty it does flaunt,
breathes life into all, a nurturing haunt,
Wrapped in a blanket, green and blue font.
nature's canvas, a beatific haunt.

Earth, a special beauty in heavenly way,
glowing with sunrise, a radiant display,
As the sun dances from east to west, a playful array,
animals and birds join, in joyous play.

Dewdrops sparkle on the verdant stage,
yet humans seek profit, ignoring nature's gauge.
Anger brewed, she rages, a furious page,
unleashing storms, a cyclonic rampage.

A symphony of life, nature's joyful run,
mountains, sea, flora, and fauna, under the sun.
Dewdrops smile, on the green carpet spun,
harmony in her arms, where all beings are one.

Where animals frolic and birds sing,
mountains stand tall, rivers in a fling.
Flora and fauna in a harmonious swing,
nature's tapestry, an eternal spring.

THE MAJESTIC STRIPES: TIGER

Within the realm of the jungle's embrace,
stripes rule on a majestic canvas,
In quiet strength, a shadow he conceives,
in moonlit glades, where the moonlight cleaves,

Majestic strides mark my way,
terror echoes in what I say.
Courage and strength in my blood,
a spirit resilient, a force understood.

For income, lives are slain,
nature weeps, a silent pain.
A dark truth that can't be denied,
In this harsh world, where values slide.

Rule's the animal domain,
freedom flowing in my reign.
Don't fear people, my pow very strong,
in my presence, resilience prolongs.

Ferocious and notorious in the cage,
ready to escape, fueled by inner rage.
Once free, unleashed from confinement,
a wild spirit, no longer in alignment.

In stripes of beauty, a tiger's grace,
hair texture gleams, a shiny embrace.
Caution in the wild, where dangers linger,
beware of hunters, the silent bringer.

THE POWER OF TIME : A POETIC EXPLORATION

Tick-tock tick-tock, the clock unwinds,
melody of movement each second binds.
In the arena of progress, my pace aligns,
no hurries, no worries, no forced confines.

I navigate with purpose, a steady fast guide,
with each challenge faced, resilience displays
It goes long when time goes wrong,
yet within the struggle, a melody's song.

Each sunrise glow, 86,400 seconds unfurl,
harmony of moments, a life in swirl.
Every pulsate, every breath, a poetic swirl,
In the rhythm of time, where wonders curl.

Use it wisely once gone, never returns,
cherish each beat before the clock grabs.
On the canvas of time, decisions unlock,
take a deep breath, as the ticking clock.

Past unfolds as history's art, present a gift,
each chapter written, engraved on time's wrist.
Future's mystery, enveloped in the unknown,
each step forth, a tale yet to be shown.

A river of time, each wave unique,
once gone, its echoes we can't speak.
An unseen force, dominating with grace,
marching at its pace, leaving no trace.

It waits for none, persistent and free,
timeless power, beyond what we see.
It marches, a force beyond our thought,
the power of time, a tale skillfully tops.

WHISPERS OF HOPE

Hope, my dearest ally,
wearing a spectrum of shades,
With every gaze, she eludes,
leaving you in patient anticipation.

In moments of adversity, when all falters,
amidst the trials of tough times,
One solace prevails, unwavering,
and that's hope, hope, and hope again.

Instilling resilience within, a beacon of hope,
granting the strength to embrace life.
Optimism blossoms with hope's presence,
no tears, no worries, in its comforting glow.

Hold on to hope, navigate life's slope,
progress is fueled by hope,
In hope, humanity resides,
light awaits in the tunnel that guides.

Hope paints a future's scheme,
a resilient ally in problem's extreme,
Breathes life into your being,
for an enduring existence, hope, keep seeing.

In the darkest night, hope takes flight,
bearing the promise of a sunlit day bright,
Within life's realm, hope finds its scope,
for where life thrives, so does hope.

Persist with hope, let miracles unfold,
listen to the saga of aspirations retold.
Silken threads of dreams, intertwined,
a resilient anthem of the hopeful mind.

BHARAT SYMPHONY

Salute to my incredible India,
with tricolour flag, saffron, white and green,
Land of different cultures and customs,
a woven riches, where myriad cultures loom.

Land of vibrant hues beneath the sun's gold,
where history's tales and legends unfold.
From Himalayan peaks to oceans wide,
India's heart beats with cultural pride.

Adorned with the Himalayan crown she wears,
with the ocean's touch at her feet so fair.
A mother to rivers, their stories she weaves,
a guardian of valleys, where life retrieves.

Mountains adorned with flora, forests, and streams,
on one side, a picturesque valley dreams.
Ethereal beauty, in every glance she shares.
a ballet of nature, a masterpiece she declares.

Lotus, our national flower's grace,
Peacock, in vibrant hues, takes its place.
Tiger, our national symbol of might,
roaming through landscapes, a majestic sight.

You, beautiful, rare, and uniquely bright,
where freedom fighters laid their lives,
Patriotism courses through your veins, it thrives.
once known as "A Golden Bird" in the light.

ODE TO A TRUE FRIEND

In friendship's garden, petals entwine,
blooms of loyalty, friendship shines.
Through storms and sunshine, hand in hand,
friendship anchors, like grain on sand.

In the orchard of true companionship,
salute to a friend, respect never slips.
Understanding flows in the veins' design,
friendship beats in the heart's constant rhyme.

A true friendship, a harmonious melody,
notes of trust and joy, boundless and legacy.
In laughter's glow and sorrows embraced,
a timeless trust, delicately traced.

In troubles faced, a friend stands near,
loyalty unwavering, in difficulty clear.
In shared thoughts, a connection weaves,
understanding flows in myriad leaves.

With every triumph and every stumble,
you stand constant, my dearest humble.
Ode to a friend, unwavering and true,
a life's treasure, forever new.

Understanding us, crafting life's grace,
making our journey meaningful, in every embrace.
Guiding us toward dream-filled streams,
as a united team, weaving vibrant dreams.

A healing balm upon life's sore,
in troubles felt, a friend, evermore.
Shouldering joy's responsibility,
creating a life, wonderfully free.

Rarity profound, a friendship's gleam,
a precious bond, like a cherished dream.
Guiding with wisdom, advice so true,
ever ready to sacrifice, a friendship to value.

For a true friend, distance holds no fear,
they'll always stand beside you, near and dear.
In moments of joy or when skies aren't clear,
their presence remains, a comfort so near.

A bond profound, steadfast and sure,
never fading, enduring evermore.
A guiding light in life's endless tide,
always there, forever by our side.

LIFE GIVES US

Life gives you bundle of happiness, take it
Life gives you opportunity, grab it
Life gives you sorrow, overcome it
Life give you promises, fulfil it
Life gives you joys, enjoy it
Life gives you challenges, face it
Life gives you character, play it
Life gives you dreams, fulfil it
Life gives you time, utilise it
Life gives you a choice, choose it
Life gives us path, explore it,
Life gives us lesson, learn it,
Life gives moments, cherish it
Life is an adventure, accept it
Life is a chess game, play it
Life is a clay, shape it
Life is mathematical problem, solve it
Life gives you a seesaw, balance it
Be grateful for life and enjoy

HARMONY'S EMBRACE: A MELODY SYMPHONY

Music, the primal love we all embrace,
an ecstasy weaving through life's space.
In the bloodstream, positive energy's chase,
dense with harmony, a cherished grace.

Healing magical power in music
gets swamped and reaches heaven
You hear it soft or loud
soothing to the heart when things go wrong

Languageless, yet emotions it conveys,
from pop to rap, in diverse arrays.
A universal rhythm, a dance it portrays,
uniting hearts in its vibrant maze.

Trumpets blaze with triumph's call,
In the grand orchestra, united all.
Woodwinds murmur secrets near,
notes that calm, dispel all fear.

Within a realm where notes entwine,
harmony's hug, a love divine.
A melodic tapestry gracefully unfolds,
whispers of music, stories untold.

No bias, it strolls, no creed it extols,
heaven on earth through unearthed notes.
Music in the mind, dance on toes, life's rebirth,
infusing life into every living thing.

Bass and drums, heartbeat's echo,
within the melody, emotions grow.
A symphony of life and grace,
chasing harmony's embrace, an endless trace.

Strings whisper tales in the moon's soft glow,
harmony's embrace, a rhythmic flow.
Echoes of emotion, a tender serenade,
in the gentle night, a symphony is made.

Bridges of connection, tenderly strummed,
chords echo in a harmonious kingdom.
Heartbeats pulse in rhythmic grace,
a timeless melody, an eternal embrace.

In life's crescendo, a blend so sweet,
unity in diversity, a melody complete.
With every stanza, tales unfold,
harmony's triumph, a melody bold.

SUNSET BEAUTY

The Sun bidding farewell with a golden kiss,
the canvas of hues creating a masterpiece in bliss.

The proud mountains waiting in the west,
for the stories to unfold and to be blessed.

Rejoicing colours performing ballet in the sky,
as daylight says its last goodbye.

The genius, Sun with radiant brushes,
to give life to the celestìal hush.

The gentle breeze carries the stories of butterflies,
delighted to share the open canvas of the sky.

As day wraps up, birds journey nature can revoke,
swaying, dancing days memories they evoke.

Dusk unfolds its vibrant hue cloak,
moon and stars elated, promise to revoke.

As the dusk hues embrace the sky,
emotions sigh,silent echo saying goodbye.

As the sinfonietta of colours slowly fade,
Stars emerge twinkling in golden parade.

GUARDIANS OF THE EARTH: NURTURING NATURE'S HEAVEN

Within this sacred, verdant sphere, life interweaves,
a sacred duty entrusted, to preserve what nature
conceives.
Mountains adorned in snow's pure embrace,
a scene so enchanting, silence takes its place.

Harmonise with each creature, whether grand or
petite,
within every gaze, a universe, tales that entreat.
Each dawn unveils the day's enchanting grace,
listening to birdsong, deciphering butterflies'
embrace.

Preserve this earthly haven, our shared birth,
united in duty, safeguarding its intrinsic worth.
A heritage of love for posterity to rediscover.
In nature's embrace, where time does hover.

Majestic trees, sentinel and wise,
whisper tales to the winds that rise.
Embracing the earth with roots so strong,
caressing the soil, where they belong.

Mountains, guardians of the land's embrace,
in vastness, they dwell with tender grace.

Safekeeping valleys in their towering might,
dancing with rivers, a harmonious sight.

Birds soar through the azure sky so high,
feathers enhancing the canvas, a beauty to spy.
Dancing and playing with clouds in the light,
a joyful symphony, their day takes flight.

Nature's beauty guards the Earth's embrace,
nurturing a canvas with tranquil grace.
A mesmerising allure, captivating all,
guardians of the Earth, answering nature's call.

SWEET AND SOUR LOCKDOWN MEMORIES

On the canvas of time, sweet and sour lockdown memories,
a fusion of solitude and nostalgia, a journey through reveries.

Days painted in different hues, joys and despair,
a bittersweet canvas, where tolerance pairs.

In quarantine quite, memories unwind,
stories of sharing, caring, courage rides.

Sun peeps through windows with a smile of gold,
a warmth that lingers, a story to unfold.

Video calls, virtual hugs, yonder smile,
linking gaps across virtual miles.

Beauteous faces behind the mask whispers softly speak,
emotional eyes expressing at its peak.

The aroma of homemade meals delights,
families warmth in candlelight.

Books on shelves, whispered solace everyday,
upgraded wisdom in lockdown's sway.

Sanitizer's ballet against the unseen viral swirls,
frontline workers present courage like a star.

The extrovert, radiant and vibrant in the crowd,
an introvert lurks in the dark, silent and proud.

Online learning, DIY projects, creativity blossoms,
music echoing on silent streets, symphony of dream
so awesome.

Sweet and sour entangled rhyme,
lockdown memories, echoes of unique time.

STUPENDOUS WOMEN

Grace intertwines in the tapestry of strength,
a woman, extraordinary in life's vibrant length.
Together, we navigate life's diverse fashion,
gracefully embracing its intricate passion.

Born with high spirit and strong heart,
managing everything smart from the start.
In life's furnaces, we burn and align,
emerging with brilliance, a resilient shine.

Powered with all the strength,
It doesn't wane at any length.
mother, wife, sister, daughter, the roles we play,
Juggling in life with all shades, day by day.

Breathing life into others, selflessly,
expecting naught in return, gracefully.
We spread our wings to soar in every field,
guardians with a shield, our care revealed.

We bring together a world where love conquers hate,
and change everyone's fate, a powerful mandate.
Labelled weak and fragile, but warriors we are,
bold and agile, navigating life's every scar.

In the symphony of strength, our stories unfold,
stupendous women, resilient and bold.
With hearts that conquer, and spirits untold,
a force unyielding, a legacy to be told.

In challenges faced, where strength unveils,
leaving a trail of resilience in life's tales.
An unbreakable superpower we hold,
stupendous women, strong and bold.

SONG OF THE SEA

The moon's reflection on the tranquil bay,
guides sailors along their nocturnal way.
Under the night's celestial art,
ocean's poetry whispers to every heart.

So, beneath the cosmic dome's embrace,
the sea weaves tales in its tranquil space.
Midst of the sand where sea meets the land,
waves hums roar a tune both soft and grand.

Under the cerulean sky, where crabs play,
beneath the sun, the waves sway, in nature's display.
Golden sands witness their playful spree,
a coastal symphony, untamed and free.

Beneath the canvas of the midnight sky,
the sea's saga unfolds, a goodbye.
Standing on the shore, beauty to behold,
Stars in hide-and-seek, their tales untold.

So let's compose the song of the sea,
In endless serenity, one can be free.
Noble whales and dolphins dance with pride,
to the rhythm of the tide, a mesmerising guide.

Ships sail gracefully, nature's melody to ride,
a symphony of the ocean, where dreams coincide.
Caressing whispers of the wind, a serene nature's
smile,
in the dance of leaves, a tranquil aisle.

LIFE'S JOURNEY

Pages turn in life's book of tales,
a journey of ups and downs, twisting trails.
Each chapter unfolds exciting stories to tell,
words written in silver and gold, a narrative swell.

With every stumble and fall, life whispers to rise,
overcoming challenges, reaching for the skies.
Spring blossoms youth, dreams as a tide,
Autumn transitions, contentment to guide.

Pages keep turning in the book of life,
embracing every moment, joy and strife.
Grab each opportunity on your trajectory,
in life's grand journey, find your way to victory.

Keep writing adventurous chapters in life's book,
thriving each day, leaving footprints to feel alive.
In this marvellous journey, simplicity is the key,
it's a voyage, not a destination, let it be.

Life's journey unfolds, a winding path so rare,
a melody of moments, a tale woven with care.
Sunrise whispers hope, a new dawn's bright song,
each step resonates, in life's symphony, strongly.

Through valleys of laughter, and mountains of strife,
we navigate the seasons, embracing every slice.
In the dance of joy and the shadow of sorrow,
life's journey unfolds, a bright tomorrow.

Challenges faced, lessons learned in the art,
a canvas of memories, etched on the heart.
So, let's sail through time, with courage in our quill,
life's journey, a poem, with verses to fulfil.

GOA:AN EDEN ON EARTH

A little dot on the map, a paradise unveiled,
land of sun kissed shores, palm trees swaying.
A heaven of tranquillity, where time stands still,
on silver sand where dreams entwined.

Diverse cultural stories untold, in the coastal heaven,
whispers of history where spices aroma in the air.
Vibrant colours painted on Goa's canvas,
a kaleidoscope of hues, where dreams amass.

You will see many whistling coconut palms,
along with beautiful cashew farms.
Relish all the authentic goan dishes,
visiting temples, churches and making a wish.

Beauty adds due to Mandovi and Zuari river,
but don't take a dive you will get shiver.
Exciting water sports on the beach,
and climb the adventure mountains, see where you
reach.

Churches and temples, echoes of devotional grace,
spiritual vibes, in the sacred grounds.
Anjuna's beats to palolem's serenity,
Tourists enjoy Goa's pure delight.

People here, friendly, colm and chilling,
laughter echoes, memories to be traced.
Goa's magic reveals in their eyes creating memories
in Goa, truly Eden on Earth.

GUIDING LIGHT: ODE TO THE UNSUNG EDUCATOR

*In the realm of the classroom, where wisdom takes
flight,
a guiding light emerges, known as the teacher's
might.
She moulds the lives of young students with care,
transforming them with knowledge, a journey rare.*

*Beside every student, a constant supportive role,
she stands firm, nurturing dreams, an unwavering
soul.
Patience in her mind, a beacon so bright,
transforming futures, casting a guiding light.*

*Within the corridor of knowledge, where wisdom
blooms,
she's a compass, guiding students to vast intellectual
rooms.
Helping them dream big, reach for the sky,
fulfilling aspirations, teaching them to fly.*

*Inspiring all to discover their inner wisdom's grace,
she sparks the flames of potential in every student's
space.
In fulfilling their dreams, she directs the theme,
a teacher's influence, a flowing, lifelong stream.*

*She's the enchantment of education, guiding with
care,
instilling knowledge to fulfil dreams in the air.
Influencing every child throughout life's stream,
an unsung hero of wisdom, in every academic theme.*

*Within the classroom, diverse methods she employs,
encouraging every child to spread their wings,
embrace joys.
Inculcating values deep within each young heart,
discipline weaved through trial and triumph, an
essential part.*

*Profound impact she weaves on every child's fate,
her influence knows no barriers, an open gate.
Every word, a golden line of wisdom's art,
Cultivating minds, leaving an indelible mark on every
heart.*

*The teacher, a beacon of wisdom's glow,
guiding students on paths they may not know.
Igniting minds to explore their boundless scope,
salute the incredible teacher, spreading hope.*

WANDERLUST ADVENTURE: ECHOES FROM TREKKING TRAIL

Mountains cradle, adventure takes flight
wanderlust trekking, reaching new height
Mountains share tales in a singing spree
echoing beauty for all to see

Mountains stand tall, valleys on the flip side,
along the trekking track, where footsteps glide.
Echoes of laughter and joy cascade,
footprints mark the trail, a journey well-made.

Thrills and excitement embraced by nature's arms,
a breathtaking journey beneath the open sky.
Winding path with twists and turns,
in each step, history unfolds with a sigh.

Sunrise paints beauty on the mountain's peak,
nature's canvas becomes exotic.
Colours dance as the day awakes,
a masterpiece of dawn, the mountain speaks.

Careful steps on paths high and low,
wonders unfold with each step's glow.
Passionate trekking, a journey's song,
enjoying every moment in nature's throng.

Wading through rivers, weaving through the forest,
climbing hills, nature's melody absorbed.
Birdsong serenades, a woodland melody,
encounters with snakes, adventure at its peak.

Ascending peaks where clouds embrace,
rocky paths, a challenge to face.
Climbers conquer, reaching new height,
nature's allure, a majestic sight.

Embrace the trail with eager feet,
nature's wonders, each step a treat.
Trekking's joy, in every stride,
a journey's bliss, where memories abide.

SEASONAL MELODIES: NATURE'S POETIC RHYTHM

Spring's gentle caress, blossoms unfurl,
summer's warmth, a sunlit world.
Autumn whispers as leaves softly fall,
winter descends with a tranquil calm.

Spring unfolds with floral blossoms,
vibrant hues paint the natural kingdoms.
Breathing life into every living thing,
nature's canvas adorned a vivid spring.

Summer's warmth blankets the earth in brightness,
a golden hue graces everything in its light.
Breathing life into every living being,
days bathed in the radiant glow of sunlight.

Autumn whispers in the rustling leaves,
nature adorns itself in changing colours.
The air carries the scent of nature's shift,
a farewell dance as leaves gently drift.

Winter's hush, a tranquil repose,
snow blankets where serenity composes.
In the gentle frost, nature's whisper weaves,
frozen landscapes adorned with glistening eaves.

Rhythmic cycles, each season unfolds,
nature's magic in stories retold.
Ever-changing, a mesmerising rhyme,
time's dance in every season's chime.

THE HARMONY OF STRENGTH: NAVIGATING MOTHERHOOD'S CHALLENGES

On life's grand stage, a pivotal role she plays,
a cluster of strength within her embrace.
Her role as a mother, resilient and bold,
navigating challenges, a story to unfold.

In her resilient heart, joys and burdens intertwine,
her love overshadows, making burdens feel fine.
Through sleepless nights, battles she contends,
the role of a mother, a story with no ends.

In life's maze of choices, she finds her way,
a mentor guiding through both night and day.
Every challenge met with unwavering grace,
an idol of strength, in every embrace.

With a melodious voice, she weaves tales,
her narrative style, precious, interest prevails.
With patience, she conquers life's stormy tide,
guiding the melody of a mother's pride.

Through tears, laughter, and tender care, she
prevails,
with inner strength, each challenge entails.
Motherhood's journey, challenges she outshines,
with boundless love, overcoming each sign.

In life's intricate maze, mothers amaze,
strength takes centre stage in multitudes ways.
Facing challenges with confidence and might,
a resilient journey through day and night.

In the rhythm of each passing day,
her strength grows in an unyielding way.
Navigating motherhood to soaring heights,
a boundless bundle of love in endless flights.

CHRONICLES OF WISDOM: OLD AGE

In life's journey, every phase holds significance,
"Chronicles of Wisdom: Old Age" with eloquence.
A silver crown adorned, experiences to unfold,
words of wisdom, a treasure trove to be told.

Metamorphosis of looks, experiences to share,
covering life's journey from youth to wear.
Wrinkles, storytellers of experiences untold,
height of wisdom, making them great and bold.

Time swiftly moves like the sunrise and set,
old age, a stage where wisdom is met.
A treasure trove of mixed feelings unfold,
wisdom's echoes resonate as years are scrolled.

Moral lessons, treasures of tales unfold,
wisdom's trove silently opens, stories untold.
Old age, evidence of varied stories,
a timeless gold, an ageless glory.

In youth's realm, dreams take their flight,
as time progresses, wisdom takes its height.
Midlife, a bustling chapter in time's gauge,
old age unfolds, a seasoned sage.

Life's journey grows exciting as old age nears,
a treasury of wisdom gathered through the years.
Wrinkles on the face, resilience in the mind,
expressions of endurance, brilliance enshrined.

OPPORTUNITY IN LIFE

Life, a game where opportunities unfold,
silently knocking at the door, stories untold.
Seize it with joy, let your spirits soar,iss it, and in
repentance, you'll explore.

Embrace the golden opportunity, don't let it slip,
awaken and persist, with every determined grip.
Follow its trail at every stage,
fight relentlessly until you conquer the cage.

Celebrate when you invite me in,
yet if you evade my gentle spin,
I extend pity, then gracefully soar,
knocking on another door once more.

Wishing not for tomorrow, seize the present day,
gather the golden chances that come your way.
Always prepared to leap with gleaming might,
for opportunities today, embrace them in full sight.

On life's journey, opportunities gently tap,
like a surprising dream, a fortuitous chap.
A silent knock, a door to open wide,
guiding you toward your goals, reaching high tide.

Golden opportunities in life, seize them soon,
before they turn to knock on another's boon.
Achieve your goals, let your dreams unfurl,
they come by chance, a dance in life's whirl.

In the passage of time, opportunities bloom,
they're possibilities, not to assume.
Every chance unlocks a new door,
seize it, make the best, and strive for more.

A SYMPHONY OF SCHOLARS: A STUDENT'S JOURNEY

In the classroom where knowledge takes its flight,
students embark on an exciting journey so bright.
With fun and adventure, their studies unfold,
eager to explore, a thirst for learning untold.

Balance your time between play and study,
no precious moments to waste, be ready.
Utilise it wisely, make each second count,
today's struggle shapes a better tomorrow's mount.

Awake with the dawn's first light,
homework awaits, a task in sight.
Limited time for joy and play,
phones grumble as time slips away.

Guided at school and within the home,
instructions echo, a constant poem.
Yet, the call to play and enjoy is rare,
amidst the persistent study affair.

School, a haven, a second abode,
moulding minds for a brighter road.
Teachers step into parental roles,
to teach and comfort, guiding youthful souls.

In the symphony of scholars, students keen,
Journey of learning, a test for the scene.
Pages filled with notes to comprehend and write,
a sea of knowledge, each lesson shining bright.

In every class, information does accrue,
scholars, eager minds, crave to learn anew.
Challenges embraced with enthusiasm,
guided by teachers, notes, and wisdom.

The student's journey, a timeless quest,
a tapestry unfolding, in learning zest.
Endless exploration, knowledge's bequest,
forever evolving, a scholar's best.

BRIDGING THE GENERATION GAP: A POETIC EXPLORATION

Through the passage of time, two generations meet,
a delicate bridge forms where perspectives greet.
Each with unique views, a blend of the old and new,
striving to understand, a bridge both build and
renew.

Wisdom from the old, shared with the young,
youth brings innovation, thinking unstrung.
Generations striving to adjust their view,
bridging gaps together on a shared page anew.

Through words, understanding finds its grace,
explaining old and new in shared space.
Together, converge on a common stand,
bridging the gap, uniting both in one strand.

Old and young converge on the same page,
understanding blossoms, a shared sage.
Each takes a step closer in this space,
a new beginning, a harmonious embrace.

Through words, bridges span the years' divide,
wisdom shared dissolves age-old fears, a guide.
Elders reminisce about days of old,
youth brings advancing skills, stories untold.

No generation labelled good or bad,
each carries stories, both happy and sad.
Different times, distinct life's theme,
In every era, dreams and struggles gleam.

A CHERISHABLE CHILDHOOD

*Faces adorned with innocence, minds full of dreams,
a magical time, where joy gleams.
Playgrounds echo with boundless energy,
a cherishable childhood, forever in memory.*

*Tiny footsteps, eager to imprint the playground's
ground,
playing games, laughter and joy abound.
Imagination running wild, crafting stories untold,
a cherishable childhood, a treasure to hold.*

*Innocent souls, delighted by garden's flowers,
playing hide and seek in leisure hours.
Ice cream treats, their favourite delight,
a cherishable childhood, pure and bright.*

*Keeping secrets to venture out and play,
skinned knees worn proudly at the end of the day.
Bedtime stories weave tales of delight,
a cherishable childhood, playing the brave role with
might.*

*Beneath the quilt, dreams bloom and grow,
serenity graces their faces in sleep's soft flow.
Every moment, a joy to explore,
cherished memories, forevermore.*

In the embrace of youth, nostalgia takes flight,
recalling the glorious days so bright.
Stored in the heart, memories unfold,
childhood's treasures, more precious than gold.

A JOURNEY CALLED LIFE

On this journey, where tales are stored,
stories of bravery, echoes forevermore.
Footprints linger, imprinted in each stride,
a journey of life's experiences, a timeless guide.

From childhood's laughter, to wisdom in old age,
youthful dreams take flight, turning life's page.
Guiding every stage with a steady light,
a journey through time, from day to night.

Navigating twists and turns with curiosity,
facing challenges, adorned with bravery.
Friendship elevates through the journey of life,
every chapter, an exciting stage, free from strife.

From sunlight till moonlight, ambition ascends,
as time passes, wisdom to great heights extends.
Life's journey, like the horizon, stretches infinite,
s continuous quest for wisdom and delight.

Adventurous journey with twists and turns,
peaks and forests, where the heart yearns.
Every journey, an adventure to bestow,
in the cascade of rain, emotions flow.

Time's journey, memories strive,
leaving footprints, a testament to life.
Every step, a chapter in the grand design,
a canvas of experiences, a story to align.

IF

"If," a mere two-letter word it seems,
yet in its essence, profound dreams.

Within its letters, potential resides,
a portal to possibilities that life provides.

If wings were bestowed, soaring through the air,
in the realm of thoughts, if the mind had eyes to bear.

If time rested in our hands, a choice to make,
pause in the past or a future journey to partake.

If wishes were seeds, a garden they could sow,
blooming into dreams, a vibrant and exquisite show.

If challenges were storms, we'd stand strong,
facing each tempest, overcoming before long.

If the mind had eyes, discerning right from wrong,
aligning things in place, harmonising the throng.

If the education system can be changed,
joy for children; no more exams, just happiness
gained.

If happiness could be bought with money,
people would have none left, no riches to be funny.

*If everything could change with a click of a button,
bedlam would ensue, chaos unbuttoned.*

61

FREEDOM

Freedom, a bird soaring in the vast, open sky,
wings unfurled, swaying with the wind's sigh.
It's the birthright of all, a universal call,
where liberty thrives and freedoms enthral.

The right to speak, a voice unbound,
a flowing river of rights, profound.
Breaking the chains of oppression's grasp,
Freedom, life's essence in a limitless clasp.

Beneath the expansive sky, dreams ascend,
voices in unity, societal norms transcend.
A chorus of liberty, breaking restrictions' chain,
rejoicing in the freedom that we attain.

Breaking the shackles of history's past,
rejoicing in freedom throughout life's vast.
The right to speak, our birthright true,
in the embrace of freedom, humanity anew.

Meeting freely, forming bonds so special,
joyful hearts, a connection beautiful.
In this space of freedom, pure and bright,
happiness blossoms, a radiant light.

In freedom, one senses expansive wings,
no boundaries constrain, a joy that springs.
Liberty embracing everything,
using it uniquely, your own way sings.

PARADISE FOR CHILDREN:GARDEN

In the floral haven where little feet frolic and play,
a paradise for children, joy in every way.
Like butterflies waltzing from flower to flower,
heaven on earth, a child's enchanting bower.

Colourful flowers and children's delight,
in the garden, both find pure joy so bright.
A green carpet where tiny feet run,
Paradise for children, endless fun.

In hide and seek, a magical realm unfolds,
wild imaginations, stories untold.
Laughter echoes in the garden's embrace,
a paradise where memories find their space.

Every flower whispers secrets untold,
in this magical garden where dreams unfold.
Blossoms and laughter together blend,
a paradise where memories eternally descend.

A realm where children roam so free,
a haven where safety is the decree.
laughter, jumps, and falls they embrace,
eager to stand, play, and retrace.

In this space, worries take flight,
a sanctuary where joy is the light.
Giggles echo, a carefree sound,
a haven for children, where happiness is found.

CONCRETE JUNGLE

In the urban sprawl, concrete dominates,
metal, sand, stones, cement collaborates.
Skyscrapers piercing the vast sky,
dreams of a house, people sigh.

War waged between trees and progress,
nature's tears, a silent distress.
Transforming jungles into cityscape,
concrete jungle, a daunting shape.

City lights paint a relentless night,
streets alive with constant flight.
But in the midst, no shade to find,
ailing Earth, a troubling bind.

Pollution rises to alarming heights,
no green haven, just concrete sights.
Traffic rushing from nowhere to nowhere,
nature's plea drowned in urban warfare.

Climate shifts, health at risk,
a concrete jungle, nature's brisk.
Earth's ailment ignored and dismissed,
in this urban sprawl, a dangerous tryst.

Rooftop gardens bloom above,
children play, their laughter and love.
Sparkling city view from on high,
metro paths twisting, turning, nigh.

Lifts and steps guide the upward climb,
different tales on each floor, a narrative rhyme.
Steel and stone weave structures tall,
concrete jungles, a beauty with a harsh call.

RAIN

Clouds darken, lightning strikes, thunder's roar,
then arrives the soft rain, a gentle downpour.
Droplets, varied in size, from large to small,
dancing with joy, a whimsical rainfall.

It taps on rooftops, a rhythmic sound,
breathing life into plants, the earth's sacred ground.
Rivers anticipate, swelling with the rainfall,
mountains yearn for a cleansing wash in its thrall.

Petrichor rises as earth drinks the rain,
mud's fragrance entices, invoking memories again.
Every raindrop, a fate to fulfil, a journey told,
fate in the ocean awaits, where destinies unfold.

On roads, puddles gleam, children delight,
paper boats sailing, streets come to life.
Rivers rejoice with rising water's song,
cascades awaken, a lively throng.

Savour each raindrop as it descends,
save every drop, life it befriends.
In each bead, stories to unfold,
a sonnet to the rain, a tale to behold.

Umbrellas aloft, raincoats adorned,
children spilled out, raindrops adorned.
A colourful scene, vibrant and bright,
Earth painted green, alive in the rain's light.

GEM OF A DAUGHTER: A POETIC TRIBUTE

In the quarry of gems, a radiant find,
a daughter, bringing life to bind.
Eyes that sparkle, an ambience so bright,
a gem of a daughter, a bond of pure light.

Her laughter echoes through the home,
breathing life into every dome.
Her smile paints the day so bright,
love treasured in her heart's warm light.

In every field, she leaves her mark,
resilient, strong, a love embark.
With kindness and a gentle heart,
wins over every heart, a work of art.

She stands tall, facing challenges with grace,
fulfilling dreams, in life's boundless space.
Unchallenged in her pursuit of success,
a masterpiece, she paints with finesse.

Ambitious, she seeks heights unknown,
facing challenges with courage, seeds sown.
Caring for each member with love,
hats off to this gem, sent from above.

A healing touch for every ailment,
her gentle hug, languages it invents.
Daughters, treasures of love so pure,
treasured with care, a bond to endure.

A special daughter, pride at every stride,
in her presence, joy becomes our guide.
Her achievements, a story to unwrap,
a daughter's pride, an everlasting map.

LIFE IS CREATIVE

On the canvas of life, myriad colours can be painted,
a palette of hues, creativity untainted.
Each step taken in the journey of creation,
crafting a masterpiece, a life of elation.

Through ups and downs in life's creative spin,
we shape it to be more creative within.
Imagination's brush paints beauty so bountiful,
in its strokes, life becomes truly wonderful.

Amid challenges faced, creativity takes flight,
life's creativity ensures overcoming each plight.
Every life experience, part of the grand scheme,
on the canvas of existence, an ever-evolving dream.

Dreams and passions blossom in life's glow,
enriching each moment, letting creativity flow.
For a fulfilling life, creativity is key,
in its vibrant hues, true fulfilment we see.

Life's beauty heightened by creativity's touch,
like a cherry atop a cake, it adds as such.
Worth in living, with colours ablaze,
for life, in its essence, is creatively raised.

Life's creativity, boundless joys it imparts,
like a painter's canvas, it captures hearts.
A mosaic of wonders, a vibrant sheen,
in every step, life's creativity is seen.

CHOICE

In life's vast arena, where paths entwine,
choices shape our journey, defining the line.
Decisions, bold and resolute,
guide us through the chapters, each pursuit.

At every junction where paths entwine,
choices beckon, decisions align.
Opt for positivity in each stride,
in the journey of choices, let hope preside.

Many possibilities to choose from the array,
each choice, a chapter in life's grand ballet.
Decisions, a crossroads where directions part,
right choices enrich, while others are lessons of
heart.

Wisely we navigate each step with care,
choosing paths that lead us where.
Decisions carve the journey, a tale to sow,
in the mosaic of choices, our destiny will grow.

In life, choices hold paramount sway,
shaping a narrative, in creativity or challenge's
display.
Decisions shape our life's intricate design,
guiding us toward the path where destinies entwine.

Options as abundant as stars in the night,
at each step, various choices take flight.
Each choice a surprise, a unique voice,
life's journey eased by every conscious choice.

PEOPLE LIKE YOU

In this world of varied attitudes, people abound,
yet, rare souls like you, kindness surrounds.
A gentle spirit, always on the go,
your laughter brings joy in life's ebb and flow.

Resilience marks every step you take,
compassion evident in every move you make.
A rare gem in the vast human sea,
people like you, a source of comfort, indeed.

Shining like a star in the vast cosmic space,
your love, unwavering, never fades.
In your presence, the world finds grace,
you make it a better, brighter place

In a world where views may differ,
people like you are a precious glimmer.
Kindness flows like a tranquil river,
with a gentle heart, you make life richer.

Your soothing touch brings comfort near,
a love unmatched, crystal clear.
In uniqueness, you stand tall,
making the world more beautiful overall.

With empathy in mind, a guiding force,
in every gesture, love takes its course.
Kindness in the heart, a nature so rare,
people like you, forever cherished and fair.

JOURNEY OF SELF DISCOVERY

In the realm of introspection's gaze,
self-discovery unfolds in myriad ways.
Exploring depths to know oneself,
seeking truths within, embracing oneself.

Emotions, a river's pure flow,
shaping identity, a journey to show.
Reflections clear, a mirror's grace, avigating toward a
better embrace.

Understanding grows with each turn,
life's journey, lessons to discern.
Original self reflected with pride,
a lifelong odyssey, where truths reside.

Discover the core of your being,
confront challenges, life's revealing.
Realisations propel you to advance,
a lifetime's journey, self-discovery's dance.
Aids in self-improvement's quest,
understanding your essence, truly blessed.
Unveiling the best version within,
self-discovery, where victories begin.
In the mirror of self-discovery's gaze,
growth and progress through positive rays.
A journey from within, strength profound,
unveiling courage where possibilities abound.

SOCIAL REFLECTION

In society, diverse hues gracefully blend,
harmony prevails, an eternal trend.
A mirror reflecting struggles and triumphs bold,
a fusion of roles, each story told.

Motivators inspire, critics may blame,
progress and setbacks, part of the game.
In this complex mix, collisions may occur,
yet, society marches, a constant stir.

Religions coexist, harmonious in tune,
a mirror reflecting the sun and moon.
Challenges arise, differing views at play,
but in this reflection, progress finds its way.

In society's reflection, diverse tales unfold,
stories of bravery, in memories, they're told.
Harmony and disharmony coexist,
voices expressing views persist.

Struggles and courage, day-to-day affairs,
a mirror reflecting hopes and despairs.
Every voice contributes to the view,
unity embraces diversity, in this mirror true.

In society's mirror, reflections profound,
a strong voice, catalyst for changes bound.
Progress brings joy to life's endless strife,
society's journey, shaped by every life.

GIRL CHILD

In the cradle of love, a girl child born,
a blossoming treasure, priceless and adorned.
Tiny in looks, many promises to keep,
in the journey ahead, proud steps to sweep.

In the human race, the girl child stands tall,
the hope of a beautiful life, the beacon of all.
Her eyes sparkle with dreams so bright,
a precious gem, the girl child, pure light.

Celebrate the foetus, no need for gender reveal,
in a world full of light, each girl's appeal.
No need for darkness, no secret to keep,
for every girl, a name to cherish and keep.

With sparkling eyes, she views the world,
bestowing hope, her banner unfurled.
Her laughter, a melody, joy impart,
a girl child's promises etched in the heart.

Her laughter echoes through every home,
advancing in time, she courageously roams.
In possibilities, success she'll find,
her presence, an auspicious moment, forever
entwined.

In little hearts, resilience stands bold,
nurtured with love, their stories unfold.
Journeys beyond imagination take flight,
many tales of empowered girls shining bright.

Girls, loving and caring by nature's grace,
deserve protection and tender embrace.
This nurturing will empower her to soar,
venturing to heights, forever wanting more.

MEMORIES UNFOLD

In the silent walk of life, memories unfold,
a cluster of thoughts, each story told.
Echoes of the past, a cluster of emotions,
guided by others or personal devotions.

Collisions of thoughts, a dance unique,
lasting a lifetime, memories speak.
Embedded in the mind, some guided, some free,
a journey through thoughts, a symphony.

Clear as crystal, emotions reside,
creating homes in hearts worldwide.
Some give joy, while others bring pain,
yet, with memories, life's journey remains.

Sweet memories, a cherished boon,
life glides smoothly under their tune.
Boosting energy, lessons they teach,
moments to cherish, within our reach.

Each memory, a gem to be treasured,
an album of memories in the mind measured.
Engraved in the heart, a tapestry of art,
nostalgia's embrace, a sentimental start.

FATHER

A steadfast presence in the family,
silent love, a protective canopy.
Guiding through shadows into light,
confronting challenges with might.

Shares responsibility in silence,
quietly guards everyone's reliance.
Without uttering a single word,
father's love, always assured.

Tears hidden, smiles bestowed,
a mentor for each winding road.
Keeping joy in everyone's view,
a father's love, strong and true.

Father and son, not always aligned,
daughter and father, a bond designed.
Son may not grasp father's love,
yet, understanding each other, they move.

Quiet strength behind every step,
a love and care that words can't intercept.
Through challenges hurled by the years,
he faces them with love, calming fears.

Always at work to meet the children's needs,
smiles return upon glimpsing the family beads.
Instilling discipline in each child's stride,
misunderstood, yet in love, he'll confide.

Amid life's hardships, his presence warms,
wisdom earned through countless years he informs.
Father's love, an eternal part,
forever cherished in the heart.

BREAKING BARRIER STORY OF RESILIENCE

In the world of challenges where barriers loom,
obstacles on the path, dispelling the gloom.
Breaking them requires courage and might,
a tale of resilience, a beacon of light.

Every challenge faced with a resilient mind,
through great efforts, solutions we find.
Each failure is a lesson to grasp,
a story of resilience, in life's every clasp.

Victories achieved tell tales of strength,
a lesson for the next generation's path.
With every hurdle crossed, resilience in sight,
guiding future paths, in the journey's twilight.

In the face of adversity, stand like a pillar,
strong and tall, resilience's thriller.
Each challenge, a new chapter to write,
a story of resilience, in courage's light.

JOURNEY BY BUS

Bustling traffic, a symphony of sound,
people chatting as the wheels go 'round.
Seats fill up, a mosaic of faces,
in this moving vessel, diverse embraces.

A sudden halt, a new chapter begins,
passengers shuffle, the journey spins.
From urban sprawls to the countryside,
on the bus, life's tapestry beside.

Conversations echo, a lively hum,
as the bus glides, destination to become.
City lights twinkle, stars in the night,
on this bus journey, emotions take flight.

The engine's hum, a soothing lullaby,
underneath the vast and open sky.
With each mile crossed, stories unfold,
a journey by bus, an experience to hold.

Bus rolling through tranquil village lanes,
advancing toward its destined terrains.
Passengers engaged in varied ways,
music hums, some dreams in the bus's embrace.

A silent road unwinding, stories unfold,
as the journey progresses, a tale to be told.
Some tapping feet to rhythmic tunes,
a bus journey, where silence and excitement croon.

WELLNESS: A GIFT TO CHERISH

In the sanctuary of wellness, a gift so rare,
treasure the essence, handle with care.
Small aches, fleeting flu, part of the ride,
maintain a positive mindset, let it guide.

Nourish your body with wholesome fare,
exercise the vessel with mindful care.
Yet, wellness extends beyond physique,
mental health, unseen but uniquely sleek.

Keep the mind fit, think thoughts that glow,
play mental games, let resilience grow.
Fuel your body with nourishing feast,
in this dual wellness, let your joy increase.

Strength for the body, resilience for the mind,
overcoming challenges, both intertwined.
A precious gift, wellness so divine,
cherish it dearly, let it brightly shine.

In the realm of health, a journey unfurls
nurture this gift, let its story be told.
Wellness, a gift of body and soul,
a treasure to cherish, make it whole.

Mind and body, a balance to dwell,
wellness, forever a precious spell.
Nurture it well, like a priceless gift,
in the journey of life, a lift.

ODES TO VEHICLES

In the realm of twists and turns,
engines awaken, a symphony begins,
Roaring sounds, vehicles forging ahead,
each journey with a purpose to fulfil.

Through the winding paths, engines hum,
motorcycles dance to their own melody,
Seasonal rides, raincoats donned for protection,
winter's chill met with jackets snug.

Cars of varied shapes and diverse brands,
gliding in tandem, swift and grand.
Maintaining safe distances with skill,
on bridges, adhering to speed limits still.

Bicycles, a great invention,
no pollution, no fuel contention.
Just pedal and savour the twists and turns,
caring for fitness, the spirit earns.

Buses, a myriad of stories to share,
each stop narrates a tale rare.
Passengers embark and alight,
journeying with joy until the destination's sight.

Trucks, robust, on highways roam,
leaving none a chance to overtake, the journey they
own.

Carrying cargo from place to place,
passionate about long journeys, they embrace.

Aircraft soaring in the sky,
a metal bird, swiftly passing by.
Taking passengers in a sublime dance,
fulfilling dreams in their airborne trance.

Ships, the sovereigns of the water domain,
courage in their hulls, facing waves, a majestic reign.
Navigating through the watery expanse,
a beautiful journey, a waterborne dance.

Vehicles, a boon to humankind,
guiding you swiftly, place to place, they bind.
Covering distances in a fleeting rhyme,
enjoy the journey, each mode a unique climb.

FLIGHT OF FEATHERS

In the vast expanse where birds touch the azure sky,
feathers gracefully rise and gently fall by.
Birds in flight, a spectacle so bright,
enjoying the joy of their majestic flight.

Soaring upwards, chasing dreams on high,
freedom embraced as they navigate the sky.
Observing the world in miniature array,
a beautiful journey in the light of day.

Waiting for dawn to take flight,
feathers light, adorning wings so bright.
Soaring in the radiant sunlight,
exploring the canvas of the beautiful sky.

Eagle, a majestic bird in its flight,
monarch of the sky, ruling with might.
Soaring to great heights in its flight,
keen eyes searching for prey, sharp and bright.

Dove, a bird of pristine white,
symbolising peace, a soothing sight.
Graceful in flight, wings unfold,
a symbol of tranquillity, stories untold.

Hummingbird with wings so slight,
a vivid palette of colours in its flight.
Feathers adorned with hues so bright,
nature's gift, a mesmerising delight.

Birds in flight with light wings soaring high,
converging with others in the sky,
Painting a vibrant canvas so bright,
their chirping symphony, a delightful bedlam.

SOCIAL GATHERING

In the garden of verses, blooms diverse,
a gathering of words, each with its universe.
Various hues, emotions they hold,
every line is a story, every tale unfolds.

When poets unite, imaginations take flight,
versatile dishes of expression, a poetic delight.
Different flavours of thoughts, in unity blend,
in this gathering, creativity has no end.

Feelings unveiled, hearts entwined,
a symphony of words, in unity bind.
A gathering of emotions, pure and sweet,
a space where hearts and verses meet.

In the social gathering where spirits come alive,
joyous laughter resonates, a festive vibe.
Conversations elevate, reaching new heights,
in the lively exchange of thoughts and delights.

Different faces, cultures, religions unite,
caring for each other, a heartwarming sight.
Friendship blossoms in this collective embrace,
a social gathering, a momentous grace.

Savouring food and drinks, a delightful affair,
strangers converging, forming bonds to share.
In this gathering, connections grow strong,
a celebration of joys, a harmonious throng.

Feet tap with joy, music resounds,
worries forgotten, in joy we're bound.
Social gathering, a realm of fun,
moments cherished, when day is done.

UNEXPECTED BIRDS DEATH

In the realm where melodies once soared,
feathers adorned, beauty underscored.
Wings that gracefully moved through space,
now in silence, a vacant embrace.

Abruptly, the chorus ceased its song,
no more echoes where joy belonged.
Feathers scattered in a mournful display,
a melody silenced, dreams decay.

The chirping halts, no bird in flight,
a stillness replacing the once vibrant light.
Mourning begins for those now gone,
in the realm of silence, life moves on.

Nature mourns the absent melody's hum,
longing for the feathered friend to come.
Tales of wings echo, forever cherished,
in the quiet, a void where joy perished.

CULTURAL TAPESTRY

In the tapestry of cultures, threads unite,
bright colours blending, a mesmerising sight.
A beautiful heritage emerges, stories entwined,
weaving narratives from each culture's bind.

The ancient thread, bold and strong,
passing down heritage, a timeless song.
Languages spoken in diverse hues,
every culture, a masterpiece, has unique views.

Every thread weaves distinct designs,
crafting hands, traditions align.
Music resonates in diverse keys,
harmony of culture, a beautiful breeze.

Festive tables adorned with diverse fare,
spices unique in each dish to share.
Heritage comes alive in every bite,
enjoying flavours, hearts take flight.

Dance marks each celebration,
a cultural tale in every gyration.
Reflecting history through choreography,
in vibrant attire, a cultural symphony.

Festivals echo the essence of culture,
expressions full of fervour.
Vibrant attires tell stories profound,
igniting the fire of cultural sound.

In the tapestry of cultures,
unity thrives in diversity's allure.
A rich fusion of stories is spun,
memories woven, beyond thoughts, begun.

PLANTS: A MEDICINAL GIFT

In nature's pharmacy,
plants, a precious gift,
Leaves, roots, and flowers too,
they are healing wonders.

In nature's realm, countless plants we find,
each a gift with healing power, intertwined.
Their verdant leaves, like emerald gems,
roots delve deep, soothing life's whims.

Chamomile, a balm for soothing calm,
lavender's scent, tranquil and warm,
Eucalyptus, breath kept rhythmic,
nature's remedies, truly a cosmic hymn.

Mint, a burst of freshness in every sip,
aloevera, guardian of our skin's grip.
Turmeric, a golden hue so bright,
nature's remedy, soothing inflammation's fight.

Blossoms bloom, health's wondrous cheer
each flowers bears a remedy clear
Botanical gift, ailments relieved
nature's embrace, healing achieved.

Plants bestowed upon us, a sacred boon,
crafting a garden, healing under the moon.
Ginger, a warm embrace in spice,
boldly flavouring life, oh, how nice!

HEARTS AGLOW : A DAY OF LOVE

In the vibes of love, a special day,
where hearts aglow and love blooms.
Arrows of love create bonds beyond compare,
Roses symbolise both old and new love.

Chocolates sweeten the moments,
expressing affection in silent eloquence.
Candlèlit dinners, a romantic embrace,
whispers of love fill the tranquil space.

Candlelit dinner, savouring moments,
expressing affection in the air.
Words of love whispering softly,
a day of love, a celebration rare.

Hand in hand, a romantic walk,
glowing moon witnesses their love.
Hearts meet, a dance of romance,
lost in each other's eyes, finding solace.

Exchange gifts, beautiful emotions,
tokens of love, expressions on faces.
Promises made, love celebrated,
a day of love, a celebration of pure.

Every moment, love to express,
memories cherished, moments to address.
Glimpses of joy in each other's eyes,
a celebration of love, priceless ties.

SIGNIFICANCE OF FLOWERS

In the kingdom of flowers, we all bloom,
but some are important, dispelling gloom.
Petals with more significance,
each blossom holds its unique brilliance.

In the morning light, daisies gleam pure and bright,
a serene beauty, a tranquil delight.
Roses, love's symbol, myriad shades unfold,
each petal tells tales of emotions untold.

Tulips stand tall, vibrant colours in the air,
swaying with the wind, a dance beyond compare.
Lilies, pure in white, a fragrant embrace,
their sweet scent enhances nature's grace.

Sunflowers stand tall in fields of gold,
turning towards the sun, their story unfolds.
Violets, calm and soothing, grace so effective,
nature's palette diverse, each flower directive.

Cherry blossoms, a brief and delicate life,
beauty beyond comparison, amidst nature's strife.
Orchids, exotic and elegant, faraway and weird,
each petal whispers tales that are revered.

A colourful flower, revered in the kingdom,
adorned at gods' feet, with medicinal emblem.
Lotus, unique among the flora,
blooms in muck, yet radiates aura.

Flowers hold importance in nature's embrace,
offered to gods, a gesture of grace.
With medicinal virtues, a healing touch,
enhancing nature's beauty, a gift as such.

DANCE: A RHYTHMIC REVERIE

In the rhythmic reverie, dance reaches new heights,
a delightful journey, a symphony of delights.
Rocking to the beats of music's sweet call,
dance unfolds in beautiful movements.

Graceful movements adorned in diverse attire,
expressive gestures convey stories entirely.
Tapping on the floor, hands speak in kind,
dance, a rhythmic reverie, captivating the mind.

Various dance forms, a spectrum wide,
from Indian traditions to Western pride.
Classical elegance to contemporary sway,
each form shines in its own unique way.

Hip-hop, an urban dance form,
full of energy, making hearts warm.
Moves and grooves creating a vibrant sight.
dance, a rhythmic reverie, an urban delight,

Folk dance, a traditional form,
celebrating culture, making hearts warm.
Sink in movements, a rhythmic delight,
dance, a captivating cultural sight.

Contemporary form, a fusion of old and new,
creating a new dance with norms askew.
Modern dance evolving, breaking through,
anybody can dance, expressing what's true.

In the dance of fitness, where life ignites,
heartbeats in rhythm, perfect beats.
Energy soaring at its highest form,
flexibility, strength, and health transform.

Dance, a beautiful expression,
universal language without words.
Moves and steps in sync with music,
a rhythmic poetry, emotions stirred.

UNEXPECTED GUEST

Unexpected guests, like a surprise,
no formal invitation or address lies.
They bring joy, spontaneity in the air,
a visit unannounced, beyond compare.

Knock on the door, a welcome surprise,
an unexpected guest, a delight in disguise.
In the warmth of home, they bring surprise,
sharing moments, laughter that never dies.

Hurriedly tidy the house, kettle on the gas,
conversation flows like water, a lively class.
Impromptu meeting, unplanned laughter heard,
uninvited, they make the home lively, every word.

Unexpected guests, ever remembered with grace,
moments created, in a short time, a joyous embrace.
A surprise meeting, where connection wins,
in the spontaneity of moments, the heart begins.

Memories created, an impromptu delight,
when guests depart, silence fills the night.
Unexpected guests, a beautiful memory,
in their surprise visit, life's sweet symphony.

Unexpected guests, a beautiful surprise,
everyone loves life's unexpected rise.
Take surprises positively, embrace with glee,
life's unexpected joys, a gift to see.

CARS: RIDING ALL HORIZONS

On a beautiful journey, roads engines strive,
cars ignite their parts to move, alive.
wheels rolling on roadbeds wide,
beginning their journey, and endless tide.

From city roads to countryside mudways,
car rides all horizons, chasing sun's rays.
Twisting and turning on different landscapes,
they come across a variety of topography, shape.

Sleek and swift, modern cars move,
covering distances, speeding, a journey to prove.
Engines hum with a melodious sound,
cars ride all horizons, adventures abound.

Many car models, each with its flair,
the king, once an ambassador, is rare.
Now lost in the latest car designs,
riding all horizons, a prestigious journey shines.

Convertible or sedan, each has its importance,
roaming through deserts and riverside, a true
essence.
Adventure at its height, wheels spinning wide,
cars ride horizons, on a thrilling ride.

Sometimes traffic jam, sometimes your own way,
cars navigate, finding their way, come what may.
Brakes and accelerators in perfect sync,
riding all horizons, a journey in a blink.

From vintage models to futuristic cars,
with the latest technology, design is like stars.
In every era, they leave their distinct mark,
riding all horizons, a journey bold and stark.

YOGA: HARMONY OF BODY AND MIND

In the realm of fitness, yoga stands supreme,
harmony of mind and body, a tranquil dream.
Rhythmic breathing, in serenity's embrace,
unity unfolds, a mindful grace.

Asanas and postures, a ballet divine,
flexibility and fitness, in every line.
A flow of postures, like a winding river,
stress releases, calmness to deliver.

Lotus position, symbolising poise,
meditation, a mindful choice.
Mindfulness blossoms with every breath,
in the garden of yoga, conquering health.

Surya Namaskar, the ultimate asana,
abundant health benefits it does span.
A full-body workout, completeness it brings,
done right, a life transformation it sings.

In Shavasana, relaxation draws nigh,
improving mental health, as peace descends.
Embrace sound sleep, a gift of tranquillity,
harmony of body and mind, forever healthy.

In the student's life, yoga finds its importance,
enhancing focus, creating a calm mental space.
Postures and breath, stress does defeat,
yoga benefits, makes studies enjoyable and retention
better.

Practice yoga everyday,
nurture both mind and body,
Health is wealth, a priceless gift,
a journey to well-being and harmony.

DANCEFIT RHYTHMS: SCULPTING WELLNESS

Physical fitness, a vital quest,
wealth of health, truly blessed.
Dance forms like aerobics, zumba delight,
flexibility, energy take flight.

Stress and stiffness melt away,
exercise becomes a joyful play.
In the rhythm of moves, fitness thrives,
aerobics and zumba sculpting lively lives.

Lively beats for aerobics flow,
heartbeats rhythm with each step's glow.
Step and jump and twirling, pure joy's embrace,
aerobic dance, a rhythmic grace.

Zumba, a fusion of dance and fitness,
moves set to exhilarating international rhythms.
Dance to the beats, sculpt wellness,
body grooves, health's rhythmism.

INNER CHILD IN YOU

In the secret chambers of your mind,
resides an inner child, pure and kind.
Innocence wrapped in a tender glow,
longing to live, alive in the flow.

Cute and innocent, the child within,
curious to know, freedom to begin.
Youthful spirit, forever free,
beautiful memories, a treasured spree.

No stress, just pure enjoyment,
basking in golden sun, embracing the rain.
Dreaming of the next day's joyous refrain,
in the cradle of childhood, memories retain.

Listening to stories of "once upon a time,"
fairy tales and dreams of princes sublime.
We grow in the cradle of innocence,
inner child, eternally pure and intense.

In the realm of maturity, the inner child is lost,
hiding in a corner, longing to be the child it boasts.
Let that inner spirit emerge, make life exciting,
embrace the child within, in every delighting.

In the heart's haven, an inner child resides,
glimpses of innocence, where joy abides.
Whispers of laughter, echoing pure and mild,
embrace the inner child, forever a cherished child.

HAPPINESS: RADIANT BLISS

In life's garden, happiness is a must,
radiant bliss bathed in sunlight and moonlight.
Heart and mind in perpetual bliss,
vibrant life thrives in happiness.

Laughter echoes from dawn till sunset,
happiness, a joy beyond comparison.
Everything aligns when joy leads,
warm friendships grow even stronger.

Happiness blooms like cherry blossoms,
radiant bliss paints smiles on faces.
Mind glows with the warmth of joy,
gratitude blooms, heart and mind are happy.

Let happiness flow through life's river,
constantly moving, like a serene flow.
Every chapter holds hidden happiness,
radiant bliss illuminates.

Happiness, the core essence of life,
life lacks colour without its vibrant hues.
As precious as a gleaming pearl,
be happy, be healthy, let joy unfurl.

GRATITUDE: BOUNTIFUL THANKS

In the grateful heart, abundance flows,
countless thanks, like a river that knows.
From dawn's first light till shadows creep,
expressions of gratitude before we sleep.

For little joys and grand delights,
a heart brimming with thankful sights.
With each inhale, with every breath,
gratitude whispers, conquering death.

In each challenge faced, gratitude reigns,
making burdens light, easing pains.
With hearts brimming with grateful delight,
winning hearts through gratitude's bright light.

In the warmth of gratitude, friends unite,
hearts expansive, creating a bond so bright.
Joy and happiness within the family grow,
abundant thanks to all, a constant flow.

HOBBY PASSION: TIME WELL SPENT

In the world of hobbies, joy takes flight,
time sweetly melts, a delight.
From brushes to paper, scissors in hand,
hobbies keep enthusiasm lively, understand.

Creativity ignites in a colourful dance,
stress-free minds, a happy trance.
Dreams planted in nature's grandeur,
embroidery crafts, patterns to savour.

Exploring nature, freezing moments in a frame,
cooking, a canvas for creative acclaim.
Adding flavours with a sprinkle of spice, obbyist
dreams elevate, oh, so nice.

Model making, a meticulous work of art,
chess pieces dance on the black and white chart.
Silent creativity, a mind engaged,
in the world of hobbies, passions are staged.

Books where characters come alive,
a literary journey takes flight, oh, so wise.
Musical instruments creating melodies sound,
hobby passion, a melodious journey profound.

From woodwork design to digital grace,
hobbies create joy in the mind's embrace.
Time spent well in the realm of creation,
hobby journey, a beautiful elation.

Hobbies bring magical moments to life,
elevating the mind above daily strife.
Joy blooms with each creative endeavour,
choose hobbies that your heart can savour.

With paper and scissors, we weave beautiful designs,
crafts come to life, without it, undefined.
The magic of hands, a hobby in mind,
creating wonders, a joy to find.

With paper and scissors, we weave designs so fine,
crafts come alive, each piece a valentine.
The magic of hands, a hobby in mind,
creating wonders, a joy to find.

Stones to collect with shapes diverse and sizes grand,
stamp collection, a unique journey, oh so unplanned.
Within the canvas of interests, passions bloom,
life's masterpiece shaped by each hobby's room.

DREAMSCAPE: JOURNEYS OF THE IMAGINATION

In the dreamscape where reality is far,
imagination at its peak, vibrant and bright.
Awe-inspiring ambiance with whispers of stars,
dreamscape blends seamlessly into the night.

Majestic ambiance with starry whispers,
dreams unfold in a regal sway.
Thoughts flow like a winding river,
in the dreamscape, where fantasies play.

Constructing castles in the air with high expectation,
soaring through the sky like free-spirited birds,
A magical realm where time bends,
in the dreamscape, where hope ascends.

Imagination at its peak,
waves of possibilities ripple through,
In the land of fantasy, minds run wild,
in Dreamscape, imagination unfurls.

Laughter in the air, happiness in the mind,
time zones blend, past and future entwined.
Confidence blossoms in this surreal space,
in Dreamscape, joy finds its place.

In Dreamscape, where thoughts ascend,
what's unreal seems real, a dreamlike blend.
Reality fades, joy in dreams unfolds,
in this wondrous realm, minds take flight, stories
untold.

REFLECTIONS OF AGE

In the mirror's gaze, time gracefully unfolds,
silver strands weave tales, stories to be told.
Lines on the face, like chapters of a book,
a reflection of age, where wisdom took.

Youthful vigour transforms to a matured grace,
a silver crown worn, an emblem of life's embrace.
Energy of youth may have taken flight,
yet, in every wrinkle, a journey's insight.

Mirror, mirror, whispers the passage of years,
each silver thread, a testament that endears.
In the quiet reflection, memories engage,
a masterpiece painted in the reflections of age.

Reflection of age, a timeless journey,
chapters left behind, memories a gurney.
Eyes eager to express stories untold,
time's passage, a tale never to unfold.

Age is but a number, a fleeting score,
the heart's rhythm keeps you lively, evermore.
Reflections of age, akin to aged wine,
a new outlook, a perspective refined.

Wrinkles emerge, tales from yesteryears,
stories of fruitful days, dispelling fears.
The child within stirs, a vibrant revive,
life's joy deepens, in moments we thrive.

OPTIMISTIC MINDSET

In the realm of an optimistic mindset so vital,
where positivity thrives, a force so vital.
Confidence blooms to face each strife,
no fear lingers in the optimistic life.

Setbacks become lessons, seeds to grow,
in the dark, optimism continues to glow.
Sunrises are possible with minds so bright,
in the optimistic mindset, they take flight.

Numerous obstacles may arise, yet hope remains,
maintaining an optimistic mindset, a challenge
sustains.
Through storms, courage surfaces with grace,
an optimistic mindset, a resilient embrace.

An optimistic mindset lights the way,
a glass half full, not led astray.
Seeds of optimism, sown with care,
reap a harvest of positivity rare.

In every challenge, the mind grows robust,
optimistic dreams elevate, in hope we trust.
Positive energy flows through every vein,
an optimistic mindset, a mindset to gain.

Optimistic minds find silver linings in adversity,
painting their lives with hues of hopeful diversity.
Patiently awaiting the arrival of better times,
smoothly navigating through life's intricate climbs.

In the storm of challenges, the optimist is vital,
patiently awaiting the dawn, their hope is survival.
Through dark clouds, they see the silver lining gleam,
in every challenge, optimism reigns supreme.

LIFE UNDER THE SEA

In the realm where sunlight can't breach,
life beneath the sea, an enchanting speech.
Corals and fish sway in the ocean's embrace,
a wondrous world hidden beneath the surface grace.

Shoals of fish move in perfect synchronisation,
gliding through currents, a fluid collaboration.
The seahorse, delicate and light,
in the submerged world, life takes flight.

In sea caves, secrets silently reside,
small fish find refuge from the ocean's tide.
Octopuses extend arms with grace,
life underwater, an enchanting embrace.

Turtles swim at their unhurried pace,
navigating currents, a rhythmic trace.
Sharks patrol with majestic might,
life underwater, a captivating sight.

Underwater life, a hidden treasure,
a world of beauty beyond measure.
Where dolphins dance and seagrasses sway,
life under the sea, a colourful stay.

Beneath the waves, life enthralling,
a harmonious dance in shared waters.
Aquatic beings in unity thrive,
underwater life, a captivating treasure trove.

STEERING THROUGH HORIZONS: A DRIVE TO REMEMBER

Amidst valleys and towering mountains,
steering through under the open sky.
Wheels in sync, a rhythmic dance,
a pleasant drive, a memory to cherish.

Mesmerising views unfold, an exotic journey,
mountains standing tall with pride.
Valleys below, a scenic beauty,
trees whispering good luck for the journey.

A long drive, collecting memories,
sunset painting the sky in golden hues.
Journey of emotions, an enjoyable ride,
wheels narrating stories at every spot.

Highways and mud roads intertwine,
changing nature's scenes on the way.
Wind blowing as dreams rise,
a drive to remember, under the open sky.

Memories engraved on every curve,
in the car, lessons of life are distinct.
Landscapes wide and narrow,
a drive to remember, steering through horizons.

FLUTTERING BUTTERFLIES

Amidst the garden's vibrant array,
colours bloom in a joyous display.
Aflutter on blossoms, wings unfurl,
delicate hues in nature's swirl.

Creatures of the air, with wings so fine,
nature's handcrafted design.
In the garden's embrace, beauty springs,
a symphony of life, nature's offerings.

Creatures of the air, with wings refined,
nature's artistry, perfectly aligned.
In the garden's beautiful scene,
nature's offerings, a buttery dream.

Born of metamorphosis' embrace,
from caterpillar crawl to the airy grace.
Nature's enchanting transformation,
Butterflies adorned in vibrant sensation.

On flowers, it lands with gentle grace,
a dance unfolding from flower to flower's embrace.
Sipping nectar, a sweet, delicate power,
the butterfly's enchanting journey hour by hour.

Brief yet intense, a fleeting trance,
any stories whispered in a delicate dance.
Eager to flutter, from place to place,
the butterfly, a transient grace.

Through meadows under the blue sky's allure,
adding beauty to nature's canvas, so pure.
Every hue delicate, a breathtaking feature,
the butterfly, nature's delicate creature.